Who Is That?

Seed Learning

Who is that?

That's my sister.

She's clapping.

Who is that?

That's my brother.

He's jogging.

Who is that?

That's my grandma.

She's stretching.

Who is that?

That's my grandpa.

He's driving.

Who is that?

That's my aunt.

She's painting.

Who is that?

That's my uncle.

He's swimming.

Who is that?

That's my dog.

She's digging.

Let's learn about Christmas.

December

Sunday	Monday	Tuesday	Wednesday	Thursday	Friday	Saturday
		1	2	3	4	5
6	7	8	9	10	11	12
13	14	15	16	17	18	19
20	21	22	23	24	(25)	26
27	28	29	30	31		

Trace the word December
and circle the date.